by Jim Edgar

with
R. D. Rosen
Harry Prichett
Rob Battles

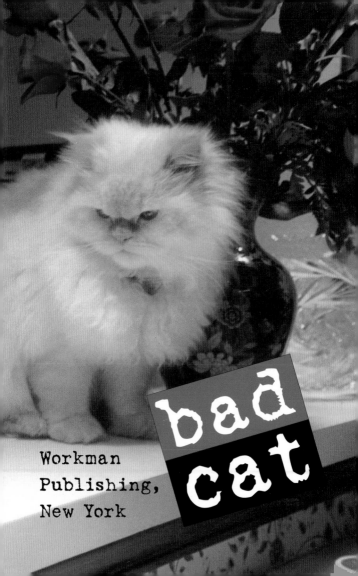

bad
cat

Workman
Publishing,
New York

Library of Congress Cataloging-in-
Publication Data is available.

ISBN 13: 978-0-7611-3619-4
ISBN 10: 0-7611-3619-3

Photo editor: John Blum

Workman Publishing Company, Inc.
708 Broadway
New York, NY 10003-9555
www.workman.com

Printed in China
First printing October 2004

20 19 18

to Marlo Menez

Acknowledgments

Jim thanks Alex, his wife
Michelle, his folks, and
Beck Hansen, another chump
from L.A. who made good.

Introduction

It is no secret that Cat owns *you*, and not the other way around. Why fool yourself with delusions of grandeur? Poor human, it's not your fault. Cat has been this way from the beginning, since the Garden of Eden. He gave the paw to Adam and Eve. He surreptitiously controlled the minds of thousands of Egyptians. He usurped Dog's position as household pet for the early Greeks. He has had his paw in the world's business for

millennia. But now Cat has had enough--enough of me, and he certainly has had enough of you.

Subconsciously, you know that inside that lovable ball of fur is a supercilious, sanctimonious, and always underestimated animal. He's not waiting to get out. He *is* out. Only perhaps you haven't noticed as you sit in your hovel littered with old pizza boxes, cigarette butts, and empty fo'ties of Schlitz malt liquor, watching reruns of *Star Trek,* petting the fluffy quadruped you have mistaken for your friend. Perhaps you need more evidence? Perhaps you are unclear about Cat's agenda?

I submit for your disapproval 244 cases in point--244 portraits of felines, their private lives laid bare by a snapshot and a few

lines. See with your own eyes
what Cat is *really* thinking,
although he offers a gentle purr
and a rub against your leg, or
what seems to be a smile in your
direction from across the room.

Want more? Then consult our Web
site, http://www.mycathatesyou.com,
where we reveal the secret
thoughts and urges of thousands
of felines in a terrifyingly
candid fashion. As for the Web
site, and the book you hold in
your hands: Kids, stay away! And
all *Homo sapiens* beware.

That is all.

Jim Edgar

"I call it *fang* shui."

NAME: Bosco
AGE: 4
HOBBY: Breeding carp

"Never mind--it's a joke
only frogs and cats would
understand."

NAME: Peanut
AGE: 1
HOBBY: Internet dating

"The few, the proud, the hairless."

NAME: Jerry

AGE: 6

HOBBY: Racquetball

"Relax--I've done thousands of these procedures."

NAME: Dotty

AGE: 8

HOBBY: Watching *Silence of the Lambs* on DVD

"Take the freakin' picture already."

NAME: Scooter
AGE: 8 months
HOBBY: Crank calls

"Chicks dig me."

NAME: Mr. Fliegel

AGE: 7

HOBBY: Collecting Charlie Parker on vinyl

"I still believe in the research we're doing here."

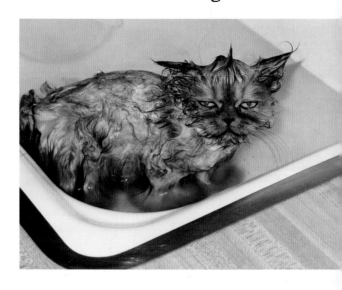

NAME: Alana

AGE: 12

HOBBY: Reading back issues of *The New England Journal of Medicine*

"Soon as the light turns green, let's see what this baby can do."

NAME: Chuck

AGE: 8

HOBBY: Collecting Beach Boys autographs

"She was naked when I came in."

NAME: Clarence

AGE: 5

HOBBY: Frequenting flea markets

"I think the play date's
over."

NAME: Rosie
AGE: 2
HOBBY: Shopping until
dropping

"Where? Where does it say 'No peeing'?"

NAME: Buckles
AGE: 2 months
HOBBY: None yet

"I assure you lobotomies are making a comeback."

NAME: Brent

AGE: 14

HOBBY: Doubles tennis

"I said no tongue."

NAME: Yvonne

AGE: 6

HOBBY: Trying new bronzers

"I remember when I was the
only cat who could juggle."

NAME: Mr. Whiskers
AGE: 15
HOBBY: Collecting Emmett
Kelly memorabilia

"Oh, yeah, baby! Oh, yeah!
I like it like that!!"

NAME: Garth

AGE: 4

HOBBY: Scrabble

"Jerry Springer called. He wants us next Friday."

NAME: Shanika

AGE: 3

HOBBY: Creating personalized scents

"Take it from me, kid--by the third show you won't even know you're naked."

NAME: Terry
AGE: 3
HOBBY: Corresponding with prisoners

"What the hell is wrong with you? *Everybody* buys Girl Scout Cookies."

NAME: Suzy

AGE: 1

HOBBY: Helping little old Chihuahuas cross the street

"The only reason I do the pageant is for the free wine."

NAME: Melissa

AGE: 5

HOBBY: Collecting placemats

"If something should happen to me, my son Damian will take over the business."

NAMES: Damian (left) and Falafel
AGES: 1 month, 2 years
HOBBIES: Nursing; darts

"I like to watch."

NAME: Paula

AGE: 14

HOBBY: Popping chondroitin
and glucosamine
supplements

"I've left you this many surprises in your sock drawer."

NAME: Rusty
AGE: 3
HOBBY: Amateur magician

"This signal means, 'Start spraying.'"

NAME: Cummerbund
AGE: 1
HOBBY: Internet poker

"You never told me you had a sister."

NAME: Alistair

AGE: 4

HOBBY: Cruising kennel corridors

"Look what I downloaded--
and it's free!"

NAME: Maxie

AGE: 1

HOBBY: Instant messaging

"Oh my god!--where are my testicles?"

NAME: Tumbles
AGE: 6 months
HOBBY: Pooping behind the dryer

"I told you the clams were bad."

NAMES: Casimir (left) and Jujube

AGES: 9 months, 4 years

HOBBY: Seafood buffets

"I charge by the
half-hour."

NAME: Wanda

AGE: 3

HOBBY: Watching QVC

"I'm feeling it. Are you feeling it?"

NAME: Larry
AGE: 6
HOBBY: Leaping unexpectedly

"My ball. First down and whatever."

NAME: Wade
AGE: 4
HOBBY: Pencil sharpening

"One step closer and
Sidney's sausage."

NAME: Muncie

AGE: 4

HOBBY: Collecting old *LIFE*
magazines

"Mmmm. Salmon smoothie!"

NAME: Foodgie
AGE: 8 months
HOBBY: Watching *Iron Chef*

"I hate playing Operation
with your drunk friends."

NAME: Barbara

AGE: 2

HOBBY: Watching the lawn

"Next round's on me, Stan."

NAME: Penelope

AGE: 10

HOBBY: Eating other cats' food

"I come from another dimension, in search of mackerel."

NAME: Flek El Danizar

AGE: 1

HOBBY: Moving small objects with his mind

"Now you know why my name is Clog."

NAME: Clog

AGE: 7

HOBBY: Working with sheet metal

"If they fed me more I could spell 'kitty.'"

NAME: Janet
AGE: 2
HOBBY: Buying too much lip gloss

37

"Have you had your fun yet?"

NAME: Gus

AGE: 5

HOBBY: Chasing dust bunnies

"Sonny says you talk too much."

NAME: Anthony
AGE: 17
HOBBY: Bocce ball

"Mrs. Claus told me to meet her here."

NAME: Alfie

AGE: 6

HOBBY: Just get me Mrs. Claus

"Blitzen's a putz."

NAME: Sarah
AGE: 11
HOBBY: Shedding

"Praise the Lord! I've been weaned!"

NAME: Niblet
AGE: 12 weeks
HOBBY: Speaking in tongues

"I'll have the burritos and a Corona Light."

NAME: Germaine

AGE: 3

HOBBY: Board games

"I think we're all making
good progress, but we have
to leave it there until
next week."

NAME: Ruth

AGE: 14

HOBBY: Egyptology

"I told you--nobody wants
to hear Billy Joel."

NAME: Stacey

AGE: 10

HOBBY: Compulsive cleaning
around the litter box

"Make it look like this."

NAME: Stu

AGE: 8

HOBBY: Drinking the water
in Mexico

"Man, thanks for leaving
the Xanax bottle open."

NAME: Creamsicle

AGE: 7

HOBBY: Having staring
contests with linoleum

"The first four times I
killed it, I swear to God I
had no idea it was rubber."

NAME: Appleby

AGE: 1

HOBBY: Browsing through
women's magazines

"I found my drink."

NAME: Laverne
AGE: 8
HOBBY: Foosball

"I used to deal catnip to the kittens at the shelter."

NAME: Snax
AGE: 13
HOBBY: Trimming ear hair

"Here's to my recent neutering."

NAME: Algernon
AGE: 1
HOBBY: Bass fishing

"Ten the hard way!"

NAME: Hartley

AGE: 6 weeks

HOBBY: Betting on college sports

"Don't ask, but Klonopin *was* involved."

NAME: James
AGE: 2
HOBBY: Taking the metal detector to the beach

"I don't need to hear about your day. Just open the can."

NAME: Delilah
AGE: 3
HOBBY: Thinking about Abraham Lincoln's hat

"Hey, do I take pictures of
you when you're on the pot?"

NAME: Mansfield
AGE: 2
HOBBY: Origami

"Hey, Lou! Mr. High Roller over here wants to know where he can find a coupla broads. Twins."

NAME: Bobby
AGE: 11
HOBBY: Rock climbing

"If you want to call us a cult, that's fine. The spaceship will be here soon."

NAME: Dick

AGE: 10

HOBBY: Neural-linguistic programming

"The gates of Hades swing wide and from the abyss comes Sassafras!"

NAME: Sassafras

AGE: 14

HOBBY: Asking if her ass is too big

"These killing sprees really take it out of me."

NAME: Roland
AGE: 5
HOBBY: Powdered milk fiend

"I would disembowel
you, but what to do with
the eight meters of
intestines?"

NAME: Lady
AGE: 1
HOBBY: Cheech & Chong
movies

"You think I'm cute?
Smell my tail."

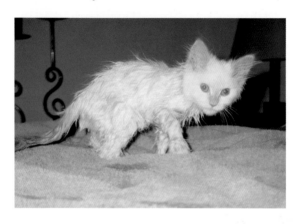

NAME: Milo
AGE: 8 weeks
HOBBY: Looking tragic

"Santa told me to tell you
to go to hell."

NAME: Bootsy
AGE: 10
HOBBY: Hating

"Can you tell I've had Botox?"

NAME: Stephanie
AGE: 12
HOBBY: Researching eating disorders

"One bag of catnip, then
I'll let you see the body."

NAME: Klaus
AGE: You're as young as you
feel
HOBBY: Having "accidents" in
the den

"Don't ever break the law
in Turkey."

NAME: Eric

AGE: 10 months

HOBBY: Customizing
scratching posts

"Got a light, sailor?"

NAME: Fay

AGE: Old enough to know better

HOBBY: What do you have in mind?

"I like a big dumb blonde."

NAME: Mike

AGE: 3

HOBBY: Candlepin bowling

"Harvey, crack me open
another cold one, will ya?"

NAME: Evelyn
AGE: 7
HOBBY: Watching Animal
Planet

"It's hard to say what
fascinates me more, the
drain or my own pathetic
life."

NAME: Ronnie
AGE: 1
HOBBY: Who cares?

"When you're through, I'd like to pee on that."

NAME: Gary

AGE: 9

HOBBY: Racing back and forth in the upstairs hall

"I think the 'shrooms are
kickin' in."

NAME: Ravi
AGE: 11
HOBBY: Following The Dead

"There's no card--how do
you know it's for you?"

NAME: Clarissa

AGE: 8

HOBBY: Nipping

"I see kidney failure in your future."

NAME: Madame Farousha

AGE: 14

HOBBY: Trances

"I lost one to a Doberman
and I chewed the other off
myself."

NAME: **J.T.**
AGE: **5**
HOBBY: Attacking strangers'
calves

"Mmmm. Blackened Mouse. A Cajun favorite."

NAME: Laura
AGE: 16
HOBBY: Bingeing on Cat Chow

"C'mon--stick your paw in the socket. I dare ya!"

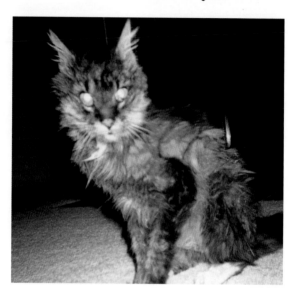

NAME: Wilson

AGE: 3

HOBBY: Reggae

"You're gonna love this place. Everyone's neutered."

NAMES: Jackie (top) and Flo
AGES: Both 4
HOBBY: Swing dancing

"From up here, I can see cleavage!"

NAME: Elmer
AGE: 2
HOBBY: Stickball

"Of course I believe it's
never happened to you
before."

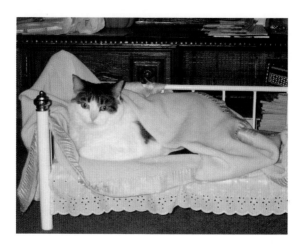

NAME: Judy
AGE: 2
HOBBY: Crystal healing

"There was nothing illegal about that hit."

NAME: Lloyd

AGE: 3

HOBBY: Cheerleaders

"If eating kittens is evil,
then, yes, I'm evil."

NAME: Wilhelmina
AGE: 4
HOBBY: Needlepoint

"It's the hairpiece that gets everyone excited."

NAME: Cliff

AGE: 13

HOBBY: Following the Arena Football League

"After I drink a fo'tie,
I am poppin' a cap in yo
ass!"

NAME: Norm
AGE: 12
HOBBY: Catfishing

"I have opposable thumbs and I know how to use them."

NAME: Hitchcock

AGE: 8

HOBBY: Tracking down his biological father

"I said *shaken*, Miss Galore, not stirred."

NAME: Otto

AGE: 10

HOBBY: Canoeing

"How many times do I have to say it? No luau."

NAME: Megan

AGE: 5

HOBBY: Collecting Fancy
Feast labels

"This yoga pose lets me
enter your room silently."

NAME: Ashaka
AGE: 7
HOBBY: Cross-stitching

"Remember to go light on
the bleach. I have a date."

NAME: Heddy
AGE: 5
HOBBY: Looking at the Lava
lamp in Sheila's room

"Oh, did I scratch your face? I'm terribly sorry."

NAME: Rikki
AGE: 2
HOBBY: Creating Thanksgiving dioramas

"This is Shelly's and my third booze cruise!"

NAMES: Shelly (left) and Dean Winkler
AGES: Both 1
HOBBY: Bridge

"Like I would know one day from another."

NAME: Abigail

AGE: 4

HOBBY: Sand art

"Holy crap. Three reincarnations and you're *still* here?"

NAME: Eddie
AGE: 3
HOBBY: Knocking over expensive objets d'art

"Yeah, I'm a half-wit. Who's asking?"

NAME: Doodles

AGE: 3

HOBBY: Humming

"Isn't it ironic that this ancient Shaolin-style move is the last thing you'll see?"

NAME: Cookie
AGE: 1
HOBBY: Casting a spell on the neighbor's dog

"It's amazing what you can see for twenty-five cents."

NAME: Mickey
AGE: 1
HOBBY: Mortal Kombat

"There was a problem in the teleportation chamber."

NAME: Anastasia

AGE: 9

HOBBY: Playing soccer with wads of paper

"Something stinks. Okay, you two--which one?"

NAME: Zanzibar
AGE: 7 months
HOBBY: Lateral leaping

"Damned Ecstasy."

NAME: Macadamia
AGE: 6
HOBBY: Collecting glow sticks

"I'm not coming out till Homeland Security tells me to."

NAME: Serafina
AGE: 4
HOBBY: Soy products

"The water's great, but the chlorine level's a tad high."

NAME: Sharlene

AGE: 11

HOBBY: Organizing kitchen drawers

"Please tell the victims'
families I'm sorry."

NAME: Smoky
AGE: 9
HOBBY: Making license plates

"Come over here. I want to show you something really cool."

NAME: Dorkhead
AGE: 2
HOBBY: Licking dinner plates

"Philly, hand me the
wirecutters."

NAME: Spengler
AGE: 8
HOBBY: Stripping furniture

"Damn--no radio."

NAME: Spanky
AGE: 5
HOBBY: Rewiring lamps

"When my kitty porn days are over, I'd like to teach ballroom dancing."

NAME: Mokey-Mokey
AGE: 2
HOBBY: The Texas two-step

"One word:
haaaaaaaaalitosis!"

NAME: Monica
AGE: 2
HOBBY: Working in pastels

"Bad cat? No, *Bat Cat*."

NAME: Blanche
AGE: 4
HOBBY: Letting people
humiliate her

"I'm not listening.
Not listening.
Can't hear you."

NAME: Sashimi

AGE: 9

HOBBY: Pitying the fool who
don't like Mr. T.

"Hey, guys—I found the erotica."

NAME: Bamba

AGE: 1

HOBBY: Getting in the lingerie drawer

"I've never even heard of Krispy Kreme. Look in the car again."

NAME: Lieutenant Feedalot
AGE: 7
HOBBY: Superhero comics

"My master went to the former Soviet Union and all I got was this lousy bust of Yeltsin."

NAME: Katnikov

AGE: 7

HOBBY: Reading Che Guevara

"That's right, Tweety—you did taw a puddy tat."

NAME: Stanford

AGE: 4

HOBBY: Slide piano

"Yes, officer, I know the routine."

NAME: Ding Dong
AGE: 2
HOBBY: Squatting

"Say that thing about my
hair balls again."

NAME: Janice

AGE: 10

HOBBY: Being a love sponge

"I think I look foxy in a
high waist."

NAME: Helene
AGE: 8
HOBBY: Sewing

"Pour some tequila into my navel and lie to me."

NAME: Lizzy
AGE: Young enough to get you in trouble
HOBBY: Sex

"That was fun. Now let's try 'whip.'"

NAME: Kevin
AGE: 2
HOBBY: Trying new cheeses

"Tell me you're sorry
again, but say it louder."

NAMES: Aquarius (left)
and Muddles
AGES: 5 months, 2 years
HOBBIES: The ball with the
little bell inside;
Greco-Roman wrestling

"Stop crying and cuff me."

NAME: Marilyn
AGE: 4
HOBBY: Decoupage

"At my age, it's nice just to cuddle."

NAME: Marmelstein
AGE: 14
HOBBY: Buying in bulk

"Last thing I remember is the fourth margarita."

NAME: Lucinda
AGE: 1
HOBBY: Urinating

"I don't know, but it has to do with recombinant DNA and a fruit bat."

NAME: Crispy

AGE: 9 weeks

HOBBY: "Drunken-style" kung fu

"Boy, do I love ear!"

NAME: Francine
AGE: 1
HOBBY: Off-season clamming

"Three words: witness . . .
protection . . . program."

NAME: Victor Two-Chins
AGE: 6
HOBBY: Ceramics

"I'm a freak? You built it."

NAME: Misty
AGE: 4
HOBBY: Sleeping in front of
heating ducts

"Wow. I've never seen ones like that before."

NAME: Brian
AGE: 3 months
HOBBY: Hiding in shoes

"Don't move, baby--I want
this lit just right."

NAME: Jerry G.
AGE: 1
HOBBY: Smoking meats

"I think it's time to go
back to rehab."

NAME: Petosky
AGE: 8 months
HOBBY: Eating freedom fries

"Too much gel."

NAME: Myrna
AGE: 1
HOBBY: Daytime soaps

"Actually, I think an all-cat production of *The Crucible* is long overdue."

NAME: Goody
AGE: 2
HOBBY: Playing the zither

"Speak for yourself. I'd still rather do *Guys and Dolls*."

NAME: Armando

AGE: 4

HOBBY: Pooping in the perennials

"I'm clown bait."

NAME: Rhoda

AGE: 4 months

HOBBY: Unicycling

"Ask me nicely or you're
not getting your pants
back."

NAME: Barley
AGE: 2
HOBBY: Wrestling inanimate
objects

"I see what you're doing--
and I like it very much."

NAME: Agnes
AGE: 12
HOBBY: Getting pedicures

"Yes, Your Honor. I do
understand the charges."

NAME: Buzzy
AGE: 3
HOBBY: Fondue

"Sure I could kill you, but that would be too easy."

NAME: Bartholomew

AGE: 17

HOBBY: Checkers

"The Three Mile Island campground? Right over there."

NAME: Sean
AGE: 9 months
HOBBY: Little League coaching

"I see London, I see France, I can see your underpants--wait--uh oh."

NAME: Klezmer
AGE: 3
HOBBY: Studying geysers

"What can I say?--he's good in bed."

NAME: Ariana
AGE: 4
HOBBY: Checking reflection in store windows

"In prison, I learned many crafts."

NAME: Happy
AGE: 9
HOBBY: Jailhouse tattooing

"Teddy and I do as we like, don't we, Teddy?"

NAME: Andrea

AGE: 1

HOBBY: Looking at motorcycle magazines

"Ken who?"

NAME: Roger
AGE: 3
HOBBY: Sardines

"Forget the donkey show.
Mojitos on the patio!"

NAME: Babs
AGE: 6
HOBBY: Making poi

"All I need now is a
bunker."

NAME: Dwayne

AGE: 5

HOBBY: Ammo

"Hold it right there. Put down the nail clippers nice and slow."

NAME: Gwen
AGE: 2
HOBBY: Using the Jedi mind trick

"This has been fun, but I'm scheduled to be spayed in half an hour."

NAMES: Sally (left) and Ethel
AGES: 4 months, 4 years
HOBBY: Mother-daughter mah-jongg

"You German Shepherds are all alike."

NAME: Antonia

AGE: 4

HOBBY: Wearing lederhosen

"Now *that's* what I call catnip!"

NAME: Steve
AGE: 8 months
HOBBY: Zoning out

"I know that everything about it is wrong, but I just can't help myself."

NAME: Wyatt
AGE: 12
HOBBY: Pilates

"No matter how often I see it, it still disgusts and excites me."

NAME: General Burnside
AGE: 1
HOBBY: Falsetto hissing

"Touch my doubloons, matey, and I'll batten down your hatches."

NAME: Cap'n Hairball

AGE: 4

HOBBY: Removing barnacles

"That's it, Fred--that's my last year working Macy's."

NAMES: Fred (left) and Homer
AGES: 8, 9
HOBBIES: Daytime television; lighting matches

"It blocks out more than harmful rays. It blocks out you."

NAME: Philippe
AGE: Don't bother me
HOBBY: Not interested

"I know he's passed out,
but his mouth is open."

NAME: Gabby
AGE: 10
HOBBY: Dipping paws in the
fish tank

"This has been a blast. Now change me."

NAME: Doug

AGE: 2

HOBBY: Skeet shooting

"Note to self: stop after third lick."

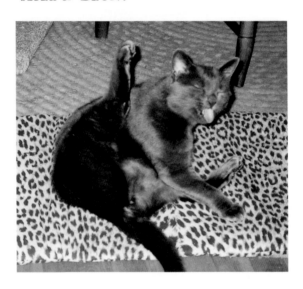

NAME: Lisa
AGE: 9
HOBBY: Flinching

"We're not laughing with you. We're laughing *at you.*"

NAME: Cardigan
AGE: 7
HOBBY: Frightening small children

"I vomited on your wallet.
Deal with it."

NAME: Perry
AGE: 1
HOBBY: Eating garbage

"My whole family's
big-boned."

NAME: Raffina
AGE: Middle years
HOBBY: Belly dancing

"Now you sleep with the fishes."

NAME: John "The Valve" O'Brien

AGE: 6

HOBBY: Lawn maintenance

"No more scurrying for you, mister."

NAME: Felix

AGE: 6

HOBBY: Collecting mouse heads

"I told you they were easy
to install."

NAME: Lance
AGE: 4
HOBBY: Canning

"You will meet a hairless
charmer and bear him six
babies. Your career is
about to take off. Avoid
Scorpios."

NAME: Marcella
AGE: 9
HOBBY: Aromatherapy

"My therapist thought it would be good for my self-esteem."

NAME: **Jasmine**
AGE: **13**
HOBBY: Nail-biting

"I'm sorry, Mrs. Carson, but these are made of plastic. I'll give you a dollar fifty for them."

NAME: Doc
AGE: 9 months
HOBBY: Making citizen's arrests

"Like **you**, this is where I do my best thinking."

NAME: Julius

AGE: 9

HOBBY: Imagining what it's like to be human

"Do *not* try that again. I eat first, then the ferret, *then* you."

NAME: Battista

AGE: 2

HOBBY: Running headlong into glass doors

"Now, class, a blow to this area will shatter the orbital bone."

NAME: Raul
AGE: 11
HOBBY: Soldering

"The one thing we miss about the carnival circuit is the drunken midget orgies."

NAMES: Sharon (left) and Karen
AGES: 6, 6
HOBBY: Trying not to breathe on each other

"Yo, yo, yo mutha! Respect this shiznit!"

NAME: D.J. Hummer

AGE: 4

HOBBY: Waiting for the Cubbies to win the pennant

"I have busts made of all my former owners."

NAME: **Fiona**
AGE: **19**
HOBBY: **Networking**

"Trust me. The plan will work. Shit on the carpet until we get tuna."

NAMES: Madeleine (left) and Drew

AGES: Both 6 weeks

HOBBY: Carpet-soiling

"Smell it. I think I
stepped in dog doo."

NAMES: Louie (left) and
Stewie
AGES: 2, 3
HOBBY: Colonial cooking

"Gentlemen, I give you my masterpiece--a high-pressure meal delivery system."

NAME: Myron
AGE: 10
HOBBY: Shortwave radio

"You're not flossing, are you, Boozer?"

NAME: Nadine

AGE: 3

HOBBY: Knocking back
jug wine

"I wish I hadn't killed the nice little doll family."

NAME: Chester

AGE: 8

HOBBY: Cop shows

"For my next impression,
I'd like to do a frittata."

NAME: Hector
AGE: 12
HOBBY: Autoharp

"The twins don't say much,
but they're very, very
thorough."

NAME: Svetlana

AGE: 3

HOBBY: Torturing ants

"He who denied it supplied it, but I'll still take a whiff."

NAME: Sebastian

AGE: 5

HOBBY: Flatulence connoisseur

"Just leave *The Watchtower* on the stoop."

NAME: Tangerine
AGE: 4
HOBBY: Vacuuming

"I'm afraid your
grandmother won't
be back."

NAME: Dominick
AGE: 4
HOBBY: Taxidermy

"This is my last show."

NAME: Mr. Moheb

AGE: 13

HOBBY: Cockfighting

"I'm through with all a
ya---you and ya stinkin',
shallow suburban lives."

NAME: Davis
AGE: 3
HOBBY: Elvis impersonator

"I hate candy. And now I hate you."

NAME: Marvin
AGE: 3
HOBBY: Light opera

"Polly want to get the hell
out of my face?"

NAME: Jennifer

AGE: 6

HOBBY: Anger management

"Listen—the farmer takes a wife, the wife takes you, *you* take the cheese, and leave me out of it."

NAME: Clancy
AGE: 6
HOBBY: Washing left front paw

"C'mon, will ya--I'm on my
break."

NAME: Sarge
AGE: Go away
HOBBY: Beat it

"What winning tickets?
These are mine."

NAME: Tito
AGE: 5
HOBBY: River tubing

"I feel sexy in my tiny sombrero."

NAME: Mitzi
AGE: 1
HOBBY: Making chili

"See? No canary."

NAME: Boz

AGE: 2

HOBBY: Baroque music

"How's it going down there? You got enough air?"

NAME: Larkin
AGE: 3
HOBBY: Paintball

"Slowly now, and I want it all in crisp tens and twenties."

NAME: "Mr. Gray"
AGE: 5
HOBBY: Collecting dried turds

"Not for all the money in the world."

NAME: Debbie

AGE: 6

HOBBY: Kabbalah

"I sent them to your
ex-wife's lawyer. Why?"

NAME: June
AGE: 8
HOBBY: Balloon animals

"I hate myself for what I
now have to do to you."

NAME: Spencer
AGE: 8 weeks
HOBBY: Spearfishing

"I have already written your obituary. It's on the counter."

NAME: Margie

AGE: 1

HOBBY: Puppetry of the ancients

"I'll need a helicopter
out of here and five pounds
of kitty litter."

NAME: Unknown
AGE: Unknown
HOBBY: Not available

"Boo."

NAME: Feldman

AGE: 10

HOBBY: Testing monocles

"You should see me when
I'm wet."

NAME: Seiji

AGE: 2

HOBBY: Biting the people who
did this

"She doesn't care if I come home drunk, and that's all I care about."

NAME: Sugar Pie Honey

AGE: 17

HOBBY: Polishing wax fruit

"Oh, that's choice!"

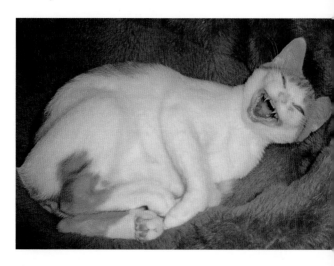

NAME: Brenda
AGE: 4
HOBBY: Old Peggy Lee
records

"All for one, one for all--
yeah, yeah, just get me
out of this hat."

NAME: Marbles

AGE: 4

HOBBY: Visiting living
history museums

"Don't shoot. Take the
wallet. It's in my left
pocket."

NAME: Cleveland
AGE: 3
HOBBY: Cursing in Spanish

"You guys get the reindeer.
The fat guy's mine."

NAMES: (left to right) Bucky,
Carrot Face, Moe, Irving
AGES: 6, 7, 1, 10
HOBBY: Holiday hijinks

"I smoke--that's why
they're yellow."

NAME: Herman
AGE: 7
HOBBY: Raising cherry
tomatoes

"Put your shirt back on."

NAME: Prince
AGE: 5
HOBBY: Bible study

"I can't wait to get out of
the Hamptons."

NAME: Mitch

AGE: 4

HOBBY: Looking at old issues
of *Maxim*

"It saw me and reared up just like this. It was definitely Sasquatch."

NAME: Andy
AGE: 8
HOBBY: Photoshop

"After this, I'll show you something really disgusting."

NAME: Melvin

AGE: 12

HOBBY: Scotch

"I love the smell of dirty underwear."

NAME: Erin

AGE: 2

HOBBY: Smelling dirty underwear

"That cheating tramp. Give
me a double."

NAME: Arnold
AGE: 5
HOBBY: Monogamy

"Give me some of that good troll lovin'."

NAME: Amanda

AGE: 3

HOBBY: Listening to American musical comedy sound tracks

"I vant to suck your blood."

NAME: Petro
AGE: 12
HOBBY: Hitchhiking

"Good god! Please don't tell me the inside of my mouth looks like that."

NAMES: Marty (left) and Brad
AGES: 1, 4
HOBBY: Texas Hold 'Em poker

"Strangest damn funeral
I've ever been to."

NAME: Oscar
AGE: 6
HOBBY: Practicing scowl

"Hey, honey! Guess whose new neighbors are nudists?"

NAME: Jim
AGE: 14
HOBBY: Getting funky

"Sorry. Private party."

NAME: Meatloaf
AGE: 15
HOBBY: Nuffin'

"I'm picking up a signal
from Minsk."

NAME: Hermione
AGE: 3
HOBBY: Googling own name

"Could I look any *less* like a cat?"

NAME: Lex
AGE: 4
HOBBY: Old postcards

"I love older women, but boy am I pooped!"

NAME: Nick

AGE: 4

HOBBY: Octogenarians

"For a can of sardines, I
go both ways."

NAME: Pat
AGE: 2
HOBBY: Welding.

"Bye Donner, bye Prancer--
next time bring more of
that excellent North Pole
weed."

NAME: Miranda
AGE: 2
HOBBY: Fantasizing about
fish

"Mom! You're home early!"

NAME: Wicky

AGE: 3

HOBBY: Assault and battery of upholstery with intent to shred

"It *smells* like Betsy Ross
slept here."

NAME: Shannon
AGE: 5
HOBBY: Social Security check
fraud

"Take a whiff and guess
what I did."

NAME: Blake
AGE: 9
HOBBY: Playing sock hockey

"Whenever I put the spider on my head, I feel irresistible."

NAME: Isabella

AGE: 3

HOBBY: Playing with own hair

"If you want me in chaps, it'll cost you another five bucks."

NAME: Dusty
AGE: 3
HOBBY: Japanese pop

"This *is* my smile."

NAME: Chaz
AGE: 7
HOBBY: Taking you for granted

"You're fired."

NAME: Donald
AGE: 9
HOBBY: Preening

"And they said smoking
crack was bad for me."

NAME: Precious
AGE: 3
HOBBY: Tearing open cereal
boxes

"What is it about our gang colors you don't like?"

NAME: Franz

AGE: 5

HOBBY: Cooking with organ meats

"Fritos, check. Twinkies, check. Bong hit, very check."

NAME: Wallace
AGE: 2
HOBBY: Tripping on the whole crazy universe

"Sure I believe in Santa Claus. Especially the meat on his legs."

NAME: Sludge
AGE: 2
HOBBY: Impressions of famous cats

"Now it's seventy-*five* trombones in the big parade."

NAME: Gus
AGE: 8
HOBBY: Vegging out

"*Now* do you understand
why I prefer Hanukkah?"

NAME: Jenny

AGE: 1

HOBBY: Making dreidels out
of clay

"It's not too late to adopt,
you know."

NAME: Soba

AGE: 8

HOBBY: Writing haiku

"I'm not a bad ass. I have a bad ass."

NAME: Owsley

AGE: 4

HOBBY: Digging himself

"You'll stop laughing
when the rest of the
brotherhood gets here."

NAME: No. 616

AGE: 9

HOBBY: Marauding

"Thank you. We'll be here all week. Try the veal."

NAME: Tony Braciole & His Two Skeletons

AGE: 7

HOBBY: Craps

"Okay, who made the hash
brownies?"

NAME: Eve
AGE: 4
HOBBY: Alternative medicine

"How was I supposed to
know what's in a Long
Island Iced Tea?"

NAME: Chi-Chi
AGE: 3 months
HOBBY: Experimenting with
unknown substances

"Love to love you, baby."

NAME: Richie
AGE: 6
HOBBY: Cologne historian

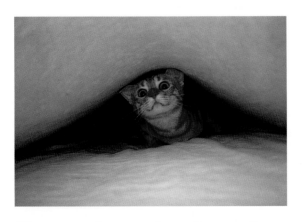

"So *that's* the 'horizontal mambo.'"

NAME: Herschel
AGE: 9 months
HOBBY: Identity theft

"I know this hasn't ended
well for you, but I still
think we've had fun."

NAME: Puff
AGE: 10
HOBBY: Iyengar yoga

About the Author

Jim Edgar lives in Seattle, Washington. He is married with no children, or cats. He pays his bills by working for Microsoft Corporation as a software engineer.

If you enjoyed these bad cats, you will find many, many more at *www.mycathatesyou.com.*